Live Your Best Life

Julia A. Royston

BK
ROYSTON
Publishing

BK Royston Publishing
P. O. Box 4321
Jeffersonville, IN 47131
502-802-5385
http://www.bkroystonpublishing.com
bkroystonpublishing@gmail.com

Cover Design: BK Royston Publishing
Cover Photo: Jonathan Snorten Photography

ISBN-13: 978-1-951941-75-8

Printed in the United States of America

Dedication

I dedicate this book to anyone who had someone else try to run your life. No one can live your life better than you. So why not start today Live Your Best Life and not someone else's.

Need help.

Turn the page.

Remember, Live Your Best Life.

Julia

Acknowledgements

First, I acknowledge my Lord and Savior Jesus Christ for giving me all of my gifts and especially my gift to write His words.

My husband who is always supportive, loving and encouraging me to utilize all of my gifts and talents. Thank you honey.

To my mother, Dr. Daisy Foree, who is my number one cheerleader and always tells me, "hang in there, you can do it." To my father, Dr. Jack Foree, who is never far away from me in spirit or my heart. I only have to look in the mirror each day to see him.

To the Envision-Radio.com family, I thank you for the opportunity and platform to share my message of love, information and inspiration. I thank every guest, my awesome production team, all who have been sharing, commenting and forwarding the information about my show, "Live Your Best Life." I thank you and pray God's blessings upon you always.

To the rest of my family, I love you and thank you for your prayers, support and love.

Table of Contents

Introduction

What does *Live Your Best Life* really mean? To me, it means being the best me that I can be for me and not anyone else. It means living in my truth and not the truth of someone else. It means living the life that I was meant to live and being okay with it deep down inside myself and not based on what others think, believe or approve. It means a lot to me. It's not always fun and sometimes it's downright scary but it's me and I'm okay with it.

Why? I only have one life to live on this earth and this is it.

I get one chance to be the best me that I can be and I'm not giving my shot, chance and/or opportunity at my best life to anyone else but me. It's a journey. I'd be lying if I got it all together or realized it on the first try. There were situations, circumstances, disappointments, failures, tries, fall downs, get back ups that happened along the way. People came and went and left again and others came along who said they were with me, had me, loved me and wouldn't leave me but they left too.

I've found subsequently my core of friends, tribe and people who really are with me and I'm good. I have the love of a great husband, mother, family and others who stand with me. In the end though, I still have the woman in the mirror to look at and the eyes staring back at me are wide open, clear and happy. I'm good. I'm okay. With God's help, I will be good and will keep moving forward to Live the Life that God died and intended for me to LIVE. Why? I get to choose and I choose me.

Finally, I want to encourage others to be their best selves as well. I give you permission to be your best at whatever that is. It is not fair for me to be my best and don't encourage you to be your best self.

So Today, Tomorrow and Always, this is Dr. Julia Royston telling you to Live Your Best Life!

Let's go!

The Faith System

"Man often becomes what he believes himself to be." Mahatma Gandhi

Let's start at the beginning. It should be the foundation on which you stand. It is hopefully what you build your life on, and that should be what you believe: your faith system. What a faith system is, in a nutshell, is what you believe in. That will probably look different for everyone who reads this book. For me, it is faith in God.

Sure, if you know me and my family, you will probably say I only believe in God because my parents told me to or I was raised in church. You are exactly correct if I was five, but, baby, I'm 57 at the writing of this book. My daddy is gone to glory, and my mama is 80 years old. As a grown woman, I believe what I want. I respect my parents; I love them with everything I have, but what I believe is what I believe. What I believe in is God! Why? Because He's really all I've got and what I know. I have experience with Jehovah God. I've prayed, shouted, laughed, cried, and trusted in this God and He has never let me down. Did I let Him down? Plenty of times, but HE NEVER LET ME DOWN. Yes, I'm yelling it to the top of my lungs with all capital letters and no editor is going to make me change it.

But for the purposes of this book, you have to believe in something other than people or you will be disappointed. Some people say a higher power and that's on you, but I know who that higher power is for me and that is God, Almighty, Jehovah Himself who keeps me moving, doing, growing, and grooving. Yes, I rhymed, but it is my truth, and I stand on it. I love Him and trust Him. I realize and know for a fact that He is the reason why I am who I am and can do what I can do and sustained the blows, hills, valleys, ups, downs, disappointments, pain, and agony of life.

I've been through many storms in my life and one of them was a marriage that I had high hopes for, along with a huge wedding, living paycheck to paycheck, trying to love my way into happiness, but it didn't happen. It was over. It took years but it happened and I grieved just like any other death. I had a great support system which I'll talk about how important that is, but the most important thing is God and my faith in Him. Although I had been raised in church and with an emphasis on faith, I didn't really know God for myself until I went through that storm. I didn't have my own relationship; my relationship was through, introduced by, and fueled by someone else: my parents and my church. But when you are placed in a city, church, and a state and with people whom you have very little connection with, you find out where your faith lies. My faith had to be tested and tried. I had to take all of the years of learning, grooming, and guidance and put it to a real-life test. I couldn't go on anyone else's word, experience, or knowledge; I had to know Him for myself. I am thankful for that. I am grateful that I have firsthand experience on deliverance. I have firsthand experience of peace in a storm. I have firsthand experience of Him bringing the right people, whom I knew not of, into my life for a reason but later to show me exactly why they were in my life. I have had experiences that no one can take from me no matter how you try.

What's your faith system? What fills the hole in your insides? What brings you peace in the storm and light in a dark and dangerous world?

What holds you together when you want to crawl under the bed and not come out for days after smelling like what for and don't come near me? It's God.

Whether you want to recognize Him or not, it's still God. Why? He said all souls are mine and He holds the world in His hands, and that includes you.

For me to live my life, I need Him each and every day of my life. Am I able to do a lot of things on my own? Sure, but it is much better when He approves, guides, leads, and instructs me on what is best to do next. My life just turns out better that way. I'm living my best life truly with God on my side, in my corner, in my ear, and guiding my feet. You should try Him. Don't take my word for it only, but you try Him for yourself. He is the best thing that happened to me, and hopefully you trust Him to bless you, too.

Again, I ask what's your faith system? It's starts with what you believe and who you believe in. Faith will be the lamp, leader, and launching pad for your life. But putting your faith in the right thing—and that's God—will be key to living your best life.

Why Am I Here?

This is probably one of the most open-ended questions and hardest ones to answer ever. I want you to take the time out of your busy day to take a hard look at yourself, your life, and what you have or have not accomplished, completed, or even started so far. The biggest part of the phrase and statement of living your best life is the word "your." It's not my life or anyone else's; it's yours. There is an afterlife after this world we have here, but right now, this is it, these are the lemons, dice, cards, or any other metaphor that you want to use to describe your life. I realize that some of you have some more descriptive and not-so-nice words to use for why you believe that you have been put on this Earth and maybe even a question mark or two, but now is the opportunity to figure it out. Why are you here? You are put here on this Earth to do what? Finally, think about that thing you do that you love and it is almost euphoric when you do it. It is something that is exhilarating and satisfying when you are able to do it.

It took me a long time to figure out why I am here. I know what I was passionate about and that was to sing. But at the writing of this book, I've just had a thyroid surgery that is still healing, and I know that I won't be able to sing for at least 6–9 months. Am I happy about it? No, I'm scared to death. Do I find joy in other things and the work that I do? You'd better believe it, overjoyed, as a matter of fact. But even though I enjoy singing, it is not the only thing that I do, and now at 57 years old, I sometimes ask myself, was singing really what I was born to do? The jury is still out, and the answer to that question is still up for grabs depending on when you met me and how long you've known me. There are some things that when I do them, like when I teach and someone understands what I'm saying and gets it, that literally take me on a high that even singing doesn't do. Teaching was a calling and something that I didn't want to do or had a passion to do it, but over the years, I have fallen in love with my calling. I am petrified every time I do it. I am always nervous and never satisfied when I am done. I know that I am called and must teach because it is also tied strategically to my business. So, in the end, I realize that teaching is really why I am here.

When God called me, His exact words were, "You shall teach my people." Really, God? That thing that my biological father said I should do and I could easily turn him down but when God says it, it WILL happen. I am a living witness. I am quite sure that many of you may or may not have had that experience of hearing God's audible voice, but He is STILL speaking. When an opportunity to do something comes to you repeatedly, over and over again, that's God. Now, I'm not talking about something illegal or immoral—get that out of your head—but you know the difference; we're adults in this space. "Gifts and callings come without repentance." If God wants you to do it, no matter how you fight it, it will happen.

The title of this chapter, "Why am I here?" is really about your purpose. First, know that finding or realizing or walking in your purpose is a journey. It doesn't happen overnight. You don't wake up one morning and say, "I'm going to find my purpose." I believe that your purpose finds you as you walk, work, and weed out what doesn't fit you. There are some items that you purchase and they actually tell you what the purpose for this product is and is not to be used for.

Why? Because some products because toxic, lethal, and deadly if used inappropriately. Have you ever used a fork to open a can? Have you have used a fork as a weapon? That's not what a fork was initially designed to do. A fork was designed to spear food, bring it closer to you on a plate, and then use that same fork to put that same food in your mouth. A fork was not designed as a weapon to harm or hurt someone, but it has been used in the past by one person or another. Often human beings have been used and misused in a manner that was not designed for a human being. There have been women, men, children of all races who have been dehumanized, tortured, beaten, and murdered, but when they were created, God created them to live, thrive, and be loved.

For you to live your best life, again, I say, not my best life but yours; you have to determine why you were born. You were born to live, thrive, and be loved, but after you have received the necessary things of life to live, there is something that you must return, give back and pull up others from their low places. That's all a part of our purpose in this life and that is to help others. But where you are supposed to fulfill that purpose is for you to walk out and find where you fit.

I can truthfully say that there is nothing like knowing, growing, and leading where I fit. This is my definition of success. I have succeeded officially when I knew what I was supposed to be doing, got in that lane, and gave it 1000% of myself. I'm all in. Now it's your turn to find out, "Why are you here?"

Why Am I Here?

_____

_____

_____

_____

_____

_____

_____

_____

_____

_____

_____

_____

_____

_____

_____

_____

_____

_____

_____

_____

Give Yourself Permission

I'm telling my age, but the old kid's game, "Mother, May I?" was kind of fun, but it always seemed like someone else was controlling your movement and ability for you to take the next steps and go further in the game. I do have control issues and I don't want to control my destiny so much that it stalls, stops, or hinders me from moving forward to live my best life. There were times in the past and even right now that I have to give myself permission to live. It starts with knowing who you are, what you are called to do, and what you are capable of doing. Next, take into account where you are right now in life and reflect on whether this is what God really intended for your life or not.

Giving yourself permission to do something else or live the life that fits you and that God designed for you is not easy. It's not just a journey, it is a choice, decision, and you may have to fight your past, people, and the future to do it. Going in a different direction as your family and friends is also not easy to do. Why? It is walking away from the familiar. It takes strength, courage, wisdom, determination, and a strong will to override what you know to walk into what you've sometimes never seen or had modeled in front of you. Since you haven't seen it before, had it modeled for you and only have a knowledge down in yourself, you'll be tempted to run back to the familiar, but I encourage you to keep walking by faith, with God's help and into the new even if you are afraid.

Some people—and this might be you—have to give yourself permission to succeed. Maybe you come from a family that didn't succeed on the level that you desire. You haven't experienced firsthand that level of success but know deep down inside that you were meant to achieve at a certain level; you have the skill to achieve at that level, and you have the discipline to achieve and maintain yourself at a certain level. You are not envious and jealous of someone else and just want what they have, but you have the actual gifts, talents, and developing abilities to perform on a certain level of life. Do it. Give yourself permission to go for it. It doesn't matter that you haven't seen in person the things you desire and are willing to work for; some things you only see with your soul's eye view, which is the will, mind, and emotions that you have on the inside and not the two eyes above your nose and on your face. It's that knower on the inside that keeps you up late at night and wakes you up earlier in the morning than everyone else to work on your dream and vision that only you and God can see and fully understand.

I've had people tease me and try to shame me into thinking that I am striving to be something that I am not and possibly living someone else's life, but at the end of the day, I've given my permission to live the life that I love, enjoy, that blesses others and, ultimately, blesses me. You are not an imposter, pretending or playing dress up in someone else' life. Yes, it's your life and that thing that makes you happy, so go for it. Mother, May I? Yes, you may give yourself permission to be all that you can be, and definitely, right now, not another minute later, Live Your Best Life.

Angels Unaware: Signs Along the Way

The Bible clearly says to be careful entertaining strangers because some have entertained angels unaware. I've had quite a few angels in my lifetime. The doctors, nurses, and teachers were definitely angels in my life, especially when I was younger. They pointed out to my parents issues that might have been temporary but still needed to be addressed with speech therapy, eye glasses, corrective shoes, and most importantly, an ear, nose, and throat specialist. Wow, the doctor bills my parents must have had. I'm living my best life now because my parents took care of some things when I was younger at the suggestion of some wonderful professional angels.

Look back over your life, no matter how old you are, and realize that God has provided people, maybe not even related to you, who have helped you on your life's journey. Be sure to reflect on how they helped you. How did they rescue you? How did they encourage you to move forward with the life that you are now living? Living your best life is just that: your whole life, the sum total, the fullest extent of your life. You didn't get to this point on your own. Someone helped you. Someone has spoken a word to you at the right time and in the right place. Someone pointed you in the right direction.

Someone else recommended you for the job or allowed you to work on their team which changed your whole life. Someone else loved you enough to let you go first.

In my life, I have had so many people protect me, direct me, and favor me so that I could get to the next level in life, as well as actually positioned me for greater exposure and onto stages that I couldn't get on by myself. Those are God's angels.

The biggest part of being given a great opportunity is that you do your absolute best. Don't half step in any way; give it everything you've got.

The angels are signs along the way that you are in the right place at the right time, and with the right spirit, you will be ushered into your next level. Along with the angels, there will be enemies, jealousy, and people who will seek to hinder your next phase, step, or move in your life, but keep positive, stay focused, and go forth in all that you desire to do and be in life.

Amazingly enough, I have had some angels who were in my life for a season. I can't remember their phone numbers or have their information to call them again. It was just for a season and not to be revisited again. It was just for that time. I love them and know that they love me, but they were not meant to be in my life forever because I may stay and not ever move forward from those people, place or time.

One of my favorite Biblical stories is of Naomi, Ruth, and Opal. Opal turned back and didn't go farther because her heart was still in Moab, but Ruth kept going and never looked back toward Moab and started a new journey, life, and love with Boaz. The love you have for the person or place may cause you to turn back; that's one reason some people can only be a bridge, cross street, or connection to the next level and not in your life permanently. No hard feelings, appreciate them and be eternally grateful for all of their help. It was one stop of the journey and not necessarily the final destination. There will be places you must go and people whom you will clearly meet who will let you know that you have met angels unawares, but they will be a sign along the way pointing you to your purpose and destiny.

At the place that they point you, at times, you must wave goodbye, never to see them again, but knowing always that they were key to you arriving safely.

Angels Unaware: Signs Along the Way

_____

_____

_____

_____

_____

_____

_____

_____

_____

_____

_____

_____

_____

_____

_____

_____

_____

_____

A Life-long Learner

I am a forever student. I may not be in school always, but I'll always be learning, every single day. I love it and appreciate each day that I learn something new. Why? It keeps me from being stagnant. It keeps me from staying in a rut and not being able to move forward. Even more importantly, it keeps me fresh, vibrant, and on the cutting edge of what is out there, especially technology. Do I buy, conform to, or incorporate everything that I learn? Heavens, no. I would be changing something each and every day or so. I would be so confused and so would my clients, but I have to know what's out there in my industry. I have to know as much about what I don't want to do as much as what I do want to do.

What have you learned new lately? What new resource, tool or, as the older people used to say, "bag of tricks"' have you added to your repertoire lately? Is it the same old, same old every single time? In 2020, I taught five sessions of my "Write that Book Now" course. It is a 10-week course where I help authors write and/or finish their books. The fourth quarter session of the course looks similar but some weeks look totally different than what I did in first quarter. Why? I learned something new about myself, my teaching style, what my clients needed, and what I should have incorporated before but kept my routine instead of changing. I learned something new about what the clients needed, so I changed on the spot. Why? Because I am the teacher and can change what I want to change. It's my class and I run it how I want to run it. I can incorporate the things that they need quickly and easily. What does that have to do with living my best life? Everything! You have to be able to adjust, adapt, switch it up, change things, and move things around to meet the needs of the people that you serve. If you are in a service job, business, and industry, it's about others and not you. Living your best life will happen to you, when you do what's best for others, and then they will take care of you. Yes! Meeting the needs of what my clients want and need is what keeps me in business, not the other way around. Doing only what I want will get and keep me broke. Hear me when I tell you that this is customer service rule #1. Give the customer what they want if at all possible. So what did you learn? Great. How do you need to change things, people, formats, systems, delivery, and distribution, etc., for your clients? Even better. Go implement, change, rearrange, and serve it up with excellence so you can do you, benefit your clients, receive payment for your services, and live your best life!

A Life-long Learner

_____

_____

_____

_____

_____

_____

_____

_____

_____

_____

_____

_____

_____

_____

_____

_____

_____

_____

_____

_____

_____

Comfortable in My Skin

I wrote a poem once and it started out, "I like me." That statement right there is a loaded one because a lot of people don't like themselves. I must confess I strived to be what other people wanted me to be for a long time. I always struggled with my weight. I was always on some type of diet. I tried to attract the right man by changing my hair constantly or shopping for the latest clothes that would fit and look nice on me. I pursued dreams, goals, and jobs that others thought I should have. I was living someone else's life, not my own, because I really didn't know what that was supposed to look like for me. Who I am and what I'm called to do and what I'm supposed to be doing and where I am supposed to be in life are things I soon found out were in God's hands and not in mine. It took a long time to get there. I wasted a lot of time doing what pleased others and looking for approval. If they liked it, I was thrilled. If they didn't like it, I was down in the dumps or a little depressed. At times, I would say things that were degrading even about myself, trying to get someone to tell me, "no, you are not like that" or "no, that's not you," to make me feel better about myself, but that is not right. There is a level of approval that you need from your boss, clients, etc., so that you can make money to provide for your household, but you can't let people control your self-esteem, self-worth, and self-image forever. Inevitably, they will control you.

The Bible says, "comparing themselves among themselves, are

not wise." [2 Corinthians 10:12 (KJV)]
Therefore, you have to decide who
you are and be the best you that you
can be and that's it. Sure, learn from
others. Take a class. Get a mentor.
Retain a coach, but at the end of the
day, you have to determine what is
best for you.

If you are not comfortable in your
abilities and who you are, the
temptation to compare, contrast, and
then compete with this same person
will overtake and consume you. We'll
never really find out who you really
are because it will get mixed up with
who someone else is, and we'll all be

confused—including you. You would think that age would bring about maturity and comfort in one's own skin but that is not always the case.

Age is a number, and high numbers don't ensure a person will automatically come to that realization. It comes differently for people and may take much for some people versus other people. Acknowledgment, acceptance of who you are and then being okay with it.

Yes, I will be working on my weight until I'm dead. I will be working on eating healthier until I'm dead, but knowing who I am as a person, I'm good. I am thankful about who God made me, allowed me to become, and afforded me the opportunity to accomplish. I'm good. I also repeat to myself over and over again, that I am fearfully and wonderfully made. [Psalm 139:14 (KJV)] Even if you do the exact same thing as someone else, it will never be delivered and/or feel or look like how you do it compared to when I do whatever God called me to do. I'm comfortable in my own skin.

Finally, the true test is when someone younger, more talented or experienced, or just has more energy comes along. You've got to resist the temptation again to be jealous, fearful, lash out, or retaliate. It shows that you are not comfortable with yourself when you fight others. Find a comfortable head space and place of peace, so that you can be okay in the skin that you are in. My husband worked for 31 years for a major corporation. There were younger people they hired whom he was old enough to be their father. He became a father figure to many because they still needed him for guidance to navigate the corporate world and advise on their careers. When my husband retired, the younger people congratulated him and appreciated him for all that he had taught them. My husband talked about how smart each and every one of them was, but they didn't have the experience, knowledge, and history with the company to be as connected as he because they didn't have the longevity. There is a place for everyone. Don't be intimidated, envious, or feeling unimportant because the light is on someone else. There will always be a place for you at the table; if not, create your own table and walk proudly in the skin that you are in.

Who Is on Your Team?

I love sports. I am about as athletic as a sloth, but I love to watch them done and done well. I love to watch team sports, football being my favorite, and also basketball, but I'll only watch baseball and/or hockey in person.

In life and especially in business, it will take a team. My core team started out as my family and friends, and they did wonderfully, but they have lives and they don't love what I do the way I love what I do. They refer me, buy products and give them away, and they are truly rooting me on to victory. I love them for it but I can't depend on them to actually work my business the way I work my business. The optimal word is "my" business. No matter how hard you try, people will not love your business as much as you should love your business. On the other hand, you are going to need people on your team, whether in volunteer or paid positions, to get the business done. Whether you are having a bake sale or own a baked goods manufacturing company, you will need help. In business, there are many hats that you may wear to get the business off of the ground and moving forward to profitability. You should be aware of every aspect of your business and done each of those tasks throughout your business cycle and sometimes, will do them all simultaneously. You cannot wear all of those hats at the same time and keep your sanity. So I ask, who is on your team?

In recent years, we have seen actual team members recruit other team members to play on their teams. Why? The team members wanted to actually play with certain people whom they got along with so they could create a great team atmosphere so they could win. In the Bible, in the story of the Tower of Babel, the people worked so well together that God Himself said, "I've got to confuse their language or these people will actually build a tower to Heaven because they had a mind to work." Wouldn't you and I love to be on that team? I would. All working for the same goal, same cause, in the same rhythm and no "weak links," just everyone in the correct position, giving it 100%, doing their jobs, pulling their weight for the same end result. Wow! What does that look like? I've been on a few teams/departments like that but very few. There is always one person whom you have to help along, talk them out of negativity, and inspire them to keep going, or you pull a little more weight so that the job can get finished on time and in excellence. I'll never forget, in graduate school, we had to be in teams of four, and three out of the four of us were scheduled to graduate at the end of the summer session. The fourth person said she didn't care about graduation and might stay in school to pursue her doctorate. The other three of us had a goal, schedules to keep, families, and other responsibilities that meant that we had to get a good grade, do well on the project, and finish in the summer—not fail and do the class over again. I had promised my parents that it would only take a year for them to help me, pay my car note and insurance while I went to school, and I was bound to keep my promise. The three of us literally had to have the "come to Jesus" talk with the fourth member so we could properly explain the importance of this class to our lives. She was late and we had to help her, but she got it done. The professor had allowed us to pick the groups, but we still had to help our team member along. Be careful whom you pick on your team. Interview them closely. Ask them about their work ethic, work schedule, and other responsibilities. Make sure that they are as committed to the project with a vested interest in getting it not only done, but done right. It matters. All of it matters. As I get older and realize time is even more precious, I am learning how to make the hard decisions that will be key to living my best life. I love everybody, but I have goals, dreams, and a purpose to fulfill. I don't have years to go around in circles, trying to decide, waiting around, then doing something halfway, and then wondering why people don't want to work with me. I'm too old. I've got this one time in my life and this is it. I don't have another 30 years to find myself and then try this and try that. I am focused, driven, and willing to invest myself, time, and money to get it done. Who is on your team? Pick wisely. Make sure they are good at what they do and not just a friend. Do they handle criticism at all? Do they gossip more than they get it done? Do they bring positive ideas to make corrective changes or do they become negative "nanny" every time that there is an issue? Life is too short. I'm too old and want to Live My Best Life here on Earth and then Forever in Heaven. Let's go! Who's ready to get it done and be on my team?

Who Is On Your Team?

_____

_____

_____

_____

_____

_____

_____

_____

_____

_____

_____

_____

_____

_____

_____

_____

_____

_____

_____

_____

Run Your Race–One Lane or Many Lanes

As a life-long learner, you will have the potential to grow and develop multiple gifts, talents, and abilities. Your career, experience, and needs of your various positions will require that you learn different things. When I taught at a private high school, I was the librarian, but they needed someone to teach technology. So I taught the Microsoft Word Suite, which I knew very well, and then I taught the website design platform, Dreamweaver. Now as much as I loved books, technology was also something that I enjoyed and loved knowing as much about as possible. My previous jobs had required a level of knowledge of technology, so I wasn't fearful and learned easily.

When I moved to my next school and new district, I had experience in two positions for the new school district and not just one. At my new school, I was the librarian for 2 ½ years and then the technology coordinator for the other 9 ½ years. So what if I had said, "no, I don't want to teach the class in technology"? I'm good right here in the library and with the job that you initially hired me for. I wouldn't have been as versatile and an even greater asset to the next position.

Staying in only one lane makes you a specialist, which is good, but over time, it can also make you expendable if that one good lane becomes obsolete. Now some specialty jobs aren't eliminated but that's not always the case, no matter how important or skilled that you need to be. There is always a possibility that you can be replaced by technology or other automation or another younger person with a different skillset and/or personality. It can happen. Times change. It is all a part of life.

I was once advised to stick to one service, product and/or type of business that I offered and not veer into other lanes, opportunities, or ventures. I didn't agree but was hesitant to start new things because I was striving to trust the person who advised. I have a stubborn streak thanks to my father and grandfather. I admit it readily. I started offering and producing what I wanted to offer and my clients wanted and needed. I'm glad that I did. Why? Because it has allowed me to be able to sustain, grow and establish other businesses because I created other lanes instead of just staying in one lane.

In track events, you have to stay in your lane for the first 200–300 meters if a race is more than 800 meters. I am not a runner. I only love to see people run, so this is only what I have observed or researched. So one lane is good for the long haul or more than 800 meters, but if you are doing short distance or a fast sprint, you have to stay in your lane. I equate this with life. There are times that you have to try out different things to see exactly where you fit. You may change lanes over the long haul, distance, and journey of life. It's not a matter of failure, unqualified or not being focused, but just the opposite: you may be finding your way to your best life and/or best you and/or best lane. Do it. Don't worry about anyone else. Run your own race so that you can live your best life. Remember, that's the goal, anyway, because at the end, you will have lived, loved, and enjoyed YOUR best life and not someone else's. So my advice to you, stay in your lane, but try out some different lanes to see if they fit. Run your race to the finish. At the end, no matter the place that you finish, you will have won!

Run Your Race—One Lane or Many Lanes

_____

_____

_____

_____

_____

_____

_____

_____

_____

_____

_____

_____

_____

_____

_____

_____

_____

_____

_____

Watch. Follow. Perform. Mentorship

I have always been very observant of people. I love it when I am able to observe people doing whatever it is that they do when they are the best at it as well as love what they do. It shows. I'm watching. I know that it is not easy, but they make it look easy when people are fulfilling their passion and purpose. Because my family members have served in various capacities in churches, community, and corporate America, I have been privileged to meet many people whom I observed and have even virtually been mentored by. Some of these great leaders I was able to meet up close and in person. It was a privilege. Since God called me to break away from some of my traditional circles in 2000 and my father's passing in 2010, I have met and been mentored by new and much different people from those I grew up with watching and being taught by. Why? I was being groomed and called to be more global and world-minded in my viewpoints. I didn't know it when I was younger, but I was taught to have the discipline to follow directions, rules, and norms and to carry out certain tasks. As I got older, God wanted me to be able to be amongst different people, cultures, religions, and faiths so that I would have this global viewpoint. Additionally, I have had business mentors and influences so that I could not only progress in my business but to also mentor others. It is important that you have someone to follow, learn from, and bounce ideas off of whom you trust and who loves you. You must pay it backward and forward to help the next generation in these same areas that you have been previously taught.

All of us will need a coach, mentor, or adviser at one point of our lives. The greatest athletes of all time in their fields needed a coach, but some coaches and athletes didn't work well together. The coach wasn't able to motivate the player and the player didn't connect with the coach. Here are a few things that I would advise anyone when seeking a mentor or coach:

1) Learn as much about them as you can before engaging them.

2) Get references and referrals and seek people out who have worked with them before.

3) Know what you want from them specifically. Don't get caught up in the light and mirrors or flashy videos or products that they offer, but ask yourself if you do need what they DO offer and are you willing and able to pay for that particular service.

4) Have a time limit. Based on your budget and information that you learn, know when you are good and need to move on to someone else or something else or nothing else. You may need time to just implement

what you've already learned before signing up for that next class or next round of coaching.

5) Be gracious, appreciative, and eat the meat/benefit/good that they gave you and spit out/ignore what doesn't work for you.

Finally, if it doesn't work, stop and exit the program. Look for someone else who will work with and for you and keep climbing higher to the level where you need to be. Don't stop until you get the help that you need to Live Your Best Life.

Clean Your Glasses and Make Sure It Fits

I always begin and end my program with Live Your Best Life, not what anybody else says, including me, but live YOUR best life. But you've got to know what that best life looks like and feels like. Sometimes it requires that you clean your glasses. What do I mean by that? Get a vision for your life. Don't compare yourself to anyone else but get a glimpse and vision for the life that you were designed to have. If you don't know, wait for it. If you have had a difficult childhood and can't see yourself happy and without turmoil, keep going, keep living, and know that you may have to find a professional to help you to work through the process.

Write down what you see. What you see for yourself should have a plan, path, and process to completion. Take inventory or stock of where you currently are and then determine what it will take to get there. You may have to get some financial advice, savings plan and/or move to another state to get it done, but don't stop until you get and live what you see for yourself.

Have you ever gone to the department store and wanted to try on an outfit that was on the mannequin? It looked great on the mannequin but when you tried it on, it didn't fit right or feel right. It looked good on the mannequin but not on you. There have been times in my life that I've felt the same way, like I was living someone else's life. At times, I was convinced that the life that someone else showed me was actually for me but the more I tried it on, tried to wear even if it came in my size, it didn't fit me. It fit someone else but not me.

Don't let anyone dictate what actually fits you, but you decide. People will see for you and tell you all kinds of things for you to be and do, but if it is NOT for you, it can get you into BIG trouble and have you living a lie. Try on and wear proudly the life that best FITS you and live it out loud and happy.

What's "fits"? Only you can answer that question. What do you see for yourself and your life? Only you can answer that question, too, but whatever it is and whatever it looks like, be sure that it is yours and that you truly, honestly, and joyfully Live Your Best Life.

Clean Your Glasses and Make Sure It Fits

_____

_____

_____

_____

_____

_____

_____

_____

_____

_____

_____

_____

_____

_____

_____

_____

About the Author

Julia Royston spends her days doing what she loves, writing, publishing, speaking, and coaching others to tell, introduce, and create ways to deliver their stories and messages to the world. That is her "Why." BK Royston Publishing LLC, Julia Royston.net, Royal Media and Publishing, and Royston Book Fairs are the conduits that she and her husband, Brian Royston, use to spread the love of reading and writing books, as well as building businesses around the world. To date, Julia has written 66 books, recorded 3 music CDs, and coached 200+ to write and publish books as well as establish their own businesses. She is the Host of the "Live Your Best Life" and the "Book Business Boss" Shows on www.envision-radio.com.

For more information, visit solo.to/juliaaroyston

Facebook @juliaaroyston

Twitter @juliaakroyston

Instagram @juliaaroyston

LinkedIn @juliaaroyston

TikTok @juliaroyston

To purchase any of Julia's books, courses or merchandise, visit:

www.roystonroyalbookstore.com

www.juliaroystonstore.com

www.bkroystonstore.com

Other Books by the Author

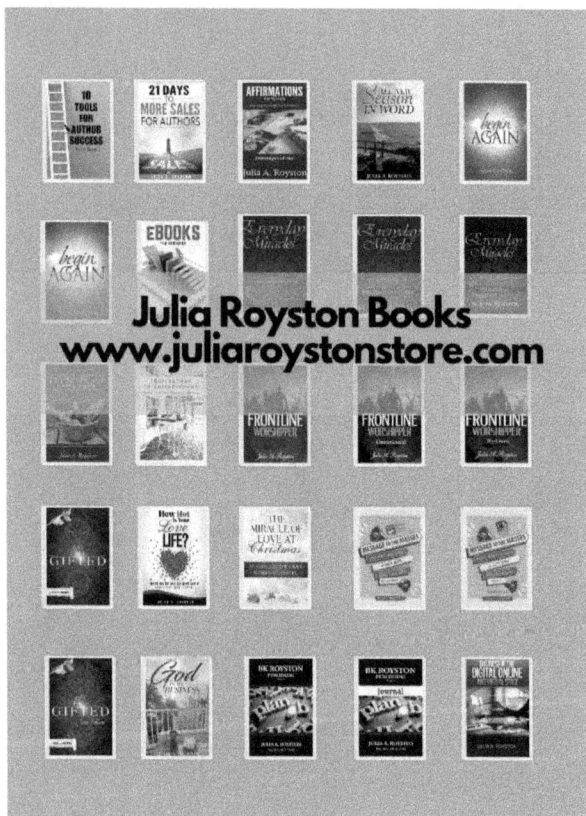

Julia Royston Books
www.juliaroystonstore.com

Other Books by the Author

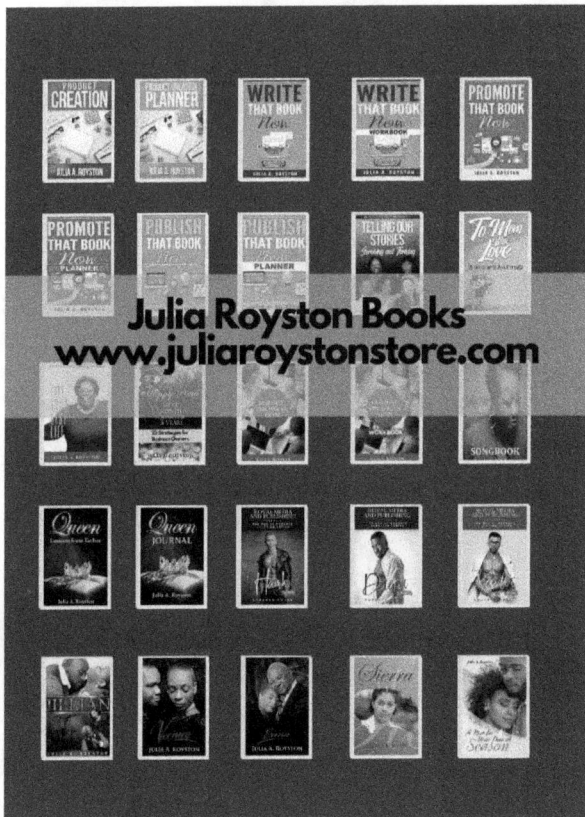

Julia Royston Books
www.juliaroystonstore.com

Other Books by the Author

Julia Royston Books
www.juliaroystonstore.com

www.ingramcontent.com/pod-product-compliance
Lightning Source LLC
Chambersburg PA
CBHW052101270326
41931CB00012B/2849